for Ralph,

WANDER-THRUSH

Lyric Essays of the Adirondacks

David Crews

Dad Crews

Nov 2018

Original versions of "On Russell M.L. Carson and *Peaks and People of the Adirondacks*," "Retreat, and a Voice for Wilderness," and "Presence, Birding, Hiking in the Woods" also published with *Adirondack Wilderness Advocates, SAGE Magazine Online,* and *Platform Review,* respectively.

Ra Press
100 Kennedy Drive #53
South Burlington, VT 05403

Cover photograph: *Lake Tear of the Clouds*
Copyright © 2016 Carl Heilman II

ISBN: 978-0-359-04301-9

ACKNOWLEDGMENTS

Thank you Brendan Wiltse and Adirondack Wilderness Advocates for publishing parts of "On Russell M.L. Carson and *Peaks and People of the Adirondacks.*" And to Caleb Northrop and the Yale School of Forestry & Environmental Studies for publishing "Retreat, and a Voice for Wilderness" in *SAGE Magazine Online.* And to Carly Susser and ARTS By the People for printing an original version of "Presence, Birding, Hiking in the Woods" in *Platform Review.*

So much of my gratitude to those individuals who offered readings of these essays, including: Stuart Bartow, Laura Bishop, David Borkowski, Ann Marie and John Crews, Dave Donohue, Joe Geddes, Willie Janeway, Laura Julier, Tom Koehler, Darryl McGrath, Craig Milewski, Ben Neville, Kate Norgard, Priscilla Orr, John Sheehan, Tyler Socash, Ed Suczewski, Marjorie Thomsen, Shane Wagner, and Brendan Wiltse.

A special thanks to Darryl McGrath and Willie C. Janeway who, not only offered readings of these essays, but were kind enough to also provide blurbs for the back cover. (What gratitude, what an honor.)

Thank you Carl Heilman II for the incredible cover photograph of *Lake Tear of the Clouds,* the highest pond-source of the Hudson River that sits at 4,293 feet above the level of the sea on a shoulder of Mount Marcy.

Thank you to the many organizations that help protect and preserve both the Adirondacks and wild spaces, including: The Northeast Wilderness Trust, The Waterman Fund, Adirondack Wild: Friends of the Forest Preserve, Adirondack Wilderness Advocates, The Adirondack Council, The Nature Conservancy, New York State Department of Environmental Conservation, New York State Adirondack Park Agency, New York State Forest Rangers, Adirondack Mountain Club, and The Forty-Sixers.

Finally, thank you dearly to Dave Donohue, Sean Tierney, and Ra Press for their care and commitment to bringing these words to the page—both with *High Peaks* as well as with these new essays. We do not consider enough how important those individuals and organizations are who support and promote the arts and letters.

CONTENTS

In visiting vast, primitive, far-off woods one naturally expects to find something rare and precious, or something entirely new, but it commonly happens that one is disappointed. Thoreau made three excursions into the Maine woods, and, though he started the moose and caribou, had nothing more novel to report by way of bird notes than the songs of the wood thrush and the pewee.

John Burroughs, "The Adirondacks"

On Russell M.L. Carson and *Peaks and People of the Adirondacks*

Why climb a mountain? Two hundred and fifty years ago the idea would have been considered absurd. Before the nineteenth century wilderness proved a place of danger. That tension drove humans into civilized communities and to venture into wilderness would soon surely prove for many reasons antithetical to human consciousness. But then, it happens. Domination or aggression, exploration and wonderment, flight in seclusion. Thoreau wrote about living deliberately.

Two detailed (and highly poetic) accounts of individuals who traveled into the remote wilderness of the Adirondacks include: T. Morris Longstreth's *The Adirondacks,* originally published in 1917, and Anne LaBastille's *Woodswoman,* published in 1976. Longstreth tells of a half year jaunt he took with his friend Lynn and their horse "Luggins," exploring on foot a huge park newly preserved by Theodore Roosevelt. LaBastille records the years spent in a small cabin she built herself—living in the woods a renewed life, manifested—with her beloved shepherd on Black Bear Lake after a quick breakup to her marriage.

Longstreth writes in his foreword, "There are but two kinds of travelers; those who enjoy the road, and those who think they will have enjoyment at the end of it. To the latter pass the time of day good-naturedly enough, but reserve the former for your company." LaBastille shares early in her story, "A withdrawal to the peace of nature might remedy my despair. I reasoned that the companionship of wild animals and local outdoor people could cure my sorrow. Most of all I felt that the creation of a rustic cabin would be the solution to my homelessness." One records a journey, the other an escape.

On a continuum it is interesting to consider these two stories as starting points: one individual viewed wilderness for the life it contained, the other saw it imbued with healing qualities. One concerned himself more perhaps with what he might see, the other how she might feel. The wilderness can move an individual

1

outward into exterior spaces, it can manifest joy. And the sublimity in solitude can retreat a person intrinsically inward, it can nurture. (Both include possibility.)

The Land

Giant of the Valley was the first High Peak to have been summited, climbed by Charles Broadhead and a survey party on June 2, 1797. Giant was also the first Adirondack mountain I ascended. (This was mostly chance.)

In 2014, when I finished hiking "The 46ers," I was one of 680 individuals who completed that year. My number (8385) was later recorded by the Adirondack Forty-Sixer organization, a number based on a final climb up Mount Marcy on the subtle morning of July 2. Since 1925, when Robert and George Marshall with guide and family friend Herbert Clark finished a seven-year expedition to climb the forty-six highest peaks in upstate New York, more than ten thousand others have continued that legacy. The word comes from the Latin *legatia*, meaning ambassador, envoy, deputy. It suggests a position of prominence. Like standing at and on top of a rock 5,344 feet above the level of the sea. I would rather like to think *heritage*, though that word comes from the Latin *heres*, meaning heir. It implies ancestry, but more connotes inheritance and ownership.

Of the forty-six High Peaks, four were originally named after men who owned the land: McIntyre, Colden, Armstrong, and Macomb (though Carson seems unclear with the true origin of Macomb). He explains, "The name Macomb marks the beginning of the historical period, for, while its date cannot be definitely fixed, it can be set as sometime between the date of General Alexander Macomb's great victory over the British at Plattsburg on September 11, 1814, and the publication of Emmons's *Natural History of New York* in 1842" (27).

Other stories—including one told by Old Mountain Phelps—

suggest the name comes from a large multi-million acre land acquisition in 1792 called Macomb's Purchase.

The land also includes Algonquin Peak, the second highest point in the state of New York at 5,114 feet above sea level, and was originally named after Archibald McIntyre, owner and operator of the local Iron Works that had been mining for iron ore until the site was abandoned in the mid-nineteenth century. In 1880, the mountain's name was changed to Algonquin Peak by Verplanck Colvin, though the name of that mountain range today still remains a variation of the original—*MacIntyre*.

Legacy, in a spiritual sense of the word, does suggest the giving or handing down of some great wisdom. To that end it feels most fitting to consider the land, the wilderness, and the experiences one has in it as a gift—always passing from one hiker to the next, always bringing people together. In fact, a legacy cannot end with any one individual. 8385 is a number on an ever-enlarging continuum expanding outward from the landscape. And there is beauty in that which is shared.

Gift has Old Norse roots with meanings like good luck. Though in later German, Dutch, Danish, and Swedish the word also connotes poison. To hike these mountains always be mindful of the gift. If it continues to move, if it is shared, it will bring luck. To possess it could mean destruction.

The Book

In the Preface of the 1973 Adirondack Mountain Club reprint of Russell M.L. Carson's *Peaks and People of the Adirondacks* (originally published in 1927 by Doubleday) George Marshall writes, "One June day in 1923, my brother Bob and I were sitting at the side of a dusty road reading letters we had picked up at the old White Lake Corners Post Office in the southern Adirondacks. Much to our surprise and delight, one included a brief historical

3

sketch of a high peak of the Adirondacks and announced an extraordinary competition. The letter was from Russell Mack Little Carson, the first Secretary of the Glens Falls Rotary Club. He had devised an original way to build membership and attendance at Rotary meetings. Each member attending one of forty-two weekly luncheons was credited with the height of one of the forty-two Adirondack peaks listed in Robert Marshall's *The High Peaks of the Adirondacks* and whoever 'climbed' the greatest number of feet on these peaks won the competition. Russ Carson added to the interest of the members by writing a historical sketch of the peak of the week" (xi).

In a letter to George's older brother Robert Marshall, on the twenty-ninth of November, 1923, Russell Carson writes of Bob's pamphlet: "It was on my desk at the office when I returned from a trip over the range last fall and no book, large or small, ever quite thrilled me as did yours. It was Longstreth's book that started me to climb Mt. Marcy and yours that obsessed me with the Adirondacks" (xii).

Robert and George Marshall, with Herbert Clark, climb Whiteface Mountain on August 1, 1918. It was the first of forty-six mountains in the region they would climb. There is a photograph of the three of them at Whiteface summit—in that cloudy sunny kind of Adirondack day—standing like gentlemen with hands at their sides, each in his respective outdoor dress: Clark in a v-neck wool sweater, Robert in a button-down lumberjack shirt, his little brother George in a long sleeve pullover, the boys with their newsy caps. Both brothers squint eyes in the sun. Robert was seventeen, his brother fourteen.

Russell M.L. Carson published *Peaks and People of the Adirondacks* in 1927, just two years after the Marshall brothers finished their epic journey. (He would be forty-three that year.) His book was an attempt to disclose the history of how each of the forty-six mountains received its name and to share the names and dates of those individuals who recorded first respective climbs. The year Carson's book was published only three individuals had stood on all forty-six peaks.

4

My first experience with Carson's text was at the Lake Placid library weeks before I myself finished hiking the 46ers. The book had marvelous history in it, a history with a new sense of the word *fact*. I never did like that word. It always felt too rigid, too aware of itself. Life is often messy, vague, ambiguous. Carson actually pieces together a broken history, presents only the information he finds, acknowledges gaps in the larger story, and offers permission for knowledge to remain fluid, evolving, like the landscape itself. He writes in the Foreword, "While every care has been taken, it is probable that there are errors in the facts gathered by a research that has had frequently to depend on human memory of old events. Readers of this volume will confer a real favour on the writer if they will call to his attention any errors which they detect, or facts which will be of value to this work if it is revised later" (lxxxv).

It pained me to have to part with the people, the anecdotes, the perspectives. What felt most fascinating was the book seemed to come in a way that connected a reader to the region's cultural heritage, the book somehow felt native to the region and its history—the story rooted in landscape, the essence of landscape conveyed in the sharing of narratives.

That is surely a romantic sentiment, one in which my ego can so easily tie. As if I, too, am somehow part of a larger oral narrative connecting back to the native people who once inhabited the land that is now my home. Me, a white suburban kid from New Jersey. Descendant of a couple of parents from Staten Island. Not colonists, but European for sure. Which, in actuality, is not far from the truth of things. How often I have longed to shed the opportunities afforded me—to feel guilt the natural way—for things I've actually done. And so to make sense I acknowledge it, intellectualize, work backwards through life. It would seem an understanding of where we have come could only better inform our awareness of the present.

My life was one in which I often felt the deep allure of the natural world—the plants and animals around me, the woods, what now has evolved into an ever-intensifying obsession for birds. Hiking comes from a stark inclination to be outside, to be in some way cut off from the world. (Thoreau is a hero.) And in today's day of social media and smarter phones and text messaging is it not ever more difficult to remain present. I hike without a phone for this very reason, and it often drives my mother to the precipice. For consciousness should make an individual more connected to place, more resolved with the land.

Carson takes us back two centuries in the settling of America. Before that, there were different people who lived here. Colony comes from the Latin *colonus*, meaning to cultivate or farm. Again, we return to ownership and control. That was the moment of disruption. To think somehow the land, and the people in it, were ours.

How to disconnect from this kind of ancestry. From a reductionist point-of-view, can being awake and living deliberately be enough? If like Thoreau I ask only for the simplest of life's offerings, if I live in such a way that allows each and every other plant, animal, and person to indeed live, if instead of luxuriating in it I promise to treat the land as though I were always a part of it—will I one day find absolution?

The People

Carson found early references to these mountains in Charles Fenno Hoffman's *Wild Scenes in the Forest and Prairie* published in 1839: "The group of hills among which the Hudson rises stand wholly detached from any other range in North America. The highest peak of the Aguanuschion range, or the Black Mountains, as some call them, from the dark aspect which their somber cedars and frowning cliffs give them at a distance, was measured last summer and found to be nearly six thousand feet in height" (8).

Moving backwards further into his research Carson uncovered

6

a New York Assembly Document dated February 20, 1838 written by Professor Ebenezer Emmons: "The cluster of mountains in the neighbourhood of the Upper Hudson and Ausable rivers, I propose to call the Adirondack Group, a name by which a well-known tribe of Indians who once hunted here may be commemorated" (9). By the nineteenth century European settlers successfully moved into a region, then named the land after the native peoples they eradicated.

The Marshall brothers, who hold the first known recorded ascent of Couchsachraga on June 23, 1924, named the forty-sixth peak after an old Indian expression which according to Verplanck Colvin recalled the vast dark wilderness beyond native settlements. Colvin was also responsible for changing Mount McIntye to Algonquin Peak and Mount Clinton to Iroquois Peak.

Santanoni Peak enters the historical and cultural discussion perhaps here. As Carson describes, "The first trails made by white men in the Adirondacks were blazed lines. 'Blaze' is said to have its derivation from the French *blesser*, meaning to wound or scar. As used in the Adirondacks it has more than a mountain-trail significance, for historically, it points a long trail back to the early French and Indian explorers who left their solitary blaze, as far as the high peaks are concerned, in the name Santanoni" (22-3).

In Emmons's *Natural History of New York,* 1842, he claimed the mountain's name was in fact "St. Anthony" corrupted into *Santanoni*. Carson continues, "The real origin of this name is obscure. Nothing can be said as to the date other than that its first known appearance in print is on a map of the headwaters of the Hudson, by William C. Redfield, accompanying his article, that was published in the *American Journal of Science and Arts* in 1838. No one knows how much older the name is or by whom it was given" (23).

A few decades after the work of Emmons a young man by the name Verplanck Colvin found himself, to say the least, quite intrigued with the Adirondack mountains. Although originally trained as a lawyer his calling was to the natural sciences and he was an individual to whom one can perhaps most attribute the saving of the Adirondack region.

According to essays and letters found in *Adirondack Explorations: the Nature Writings of Verplanck Colvin* (edited by Paul A. Schaefer) after beginning survey explorations of the Adirondack region around 1865—citing one unbelievable ascent in the Seward Range in which the hiking party was lost in a snowstorm for a great ordeal—Colvin repeatedly sent letters warning the state government in Albany that if logging and deforestation continued at the same high rate the lack of tree cover in the region would cause the snowmelt to occur too rapidly and the cities of Albany and New York would run out of water. In 1872, the state government gave Colvin ten hundred dollars to survey the region. (1872 was also the year Ulysses S. Grant signed into law the first national park of the United States of America, a park that would be named after the yellow rock walls that cathedraled it.)

At this time, in the wake of the Civil War, where battles like Gettysburg were decided by the difference in just hundreds of feet in elevation, there was a great need for topographical mapping of the land. Interestingly enough, this is around the same time curiosity and wonderment in the natural world began to evolve into ideas of ecology and conservation—a response to the growing industrialization of the nation. Colvin finds himself in the company of early nature advocates like Henry David Thoreau, Clarence King, John Muir, Charles Ernest Fay, Harriet Hemenway, and John Burroughs, who would eventually give way to the next generation of policy makers like Theodore Roosevelt and Gifford Pinchot.

When President McKinley was shot in 1901, six months into his second term, Vice President Theodore Roosevelt was informed of the news while hiking near the summit of Mount Marcy. His location: Lake Tear of the Clouds, a small pond named by Verplanck Colvin in 1872 that sits on the shoulder of Mount Marcy at 4,322 feet above the level of the sea and was discovered to be the source of the Hudson River.

8

Colvin's work was preceded by that of New York State geologist Ebenezer Emmons, Professor of Chemistry at Williams College, who was commissioned in 1837 to develop early surveys of the mountainous region in northern New York. Their definitive objective: to declare the source of the Hudson River as well as ascend a number of peaks. One notable meteorologist, William C. Redfield, played a major role in that exploration. Many parts of his journal provided important details on their work and findings. (Redfield is known for the recognition of counter-clockwise rotation in tropical storm systems.)

On August 5, 1837, the group, under the direction of Emmons and Redfield, completed the first ascent of Mount Marcy, declaring a new name at the summit in honor of the Governor at the time, William Learned Marcy.

Of the forty-six High Peaks, six remain named for politicians: Marcy, Dix, Seward, Wright, Seymour, and South Dix (though there was a recent movement to rename the last Carson Peak). Six others are named for individuals who made significant contributions to science and the arts: Gray (botanist), Redfield (meteorologist), Street (writer, poet), Colvin (surveyor), Donaldson (writer, historian), Emmons (professor).

Later that year, after news of the exploration up Marcy, author and poet Charles Fenno Hoffman found himself greatly attracted to the region. The name "Tahawus" made its first appearance in Hoffman's book, *Wild Scenes in the Forests and Prairie*. (The name can also be found on a plaque at Marcy's summit.) In Seneca-Iroquois the name translates to "He splits the sky." Further Seneca names for the mountain include: *She-gwi-en-dank-we* ("A hanging spear"), *Tu-ne-sas-sah* ("A place of pebbles"), *Kos-kong-sha-de* ("Broken water"), *Twen-un-ga-sko* ("A raised voice").

In 1908, Alfred L. Donaldson wrote for the Victory Mountain Park Committee, "The Song of Tahawus":

I am tallest of the mountains where the many mountains rise—
I am Cleaver of the Cloudland and the Splitter of the Skies—
I am keeper of the caverns where the God of Thunder sleeps—

I am older than the waters that once hid me in their deeps.

For the eyes I hold the visions of the things that make men whole—
Of the woodlands and the waters that can whisper to the soul.
In the winter robed in whiteness, in the summer garbed in green,
I am warden of the wonders of an ever shifting scene.

I am guardian of the goblet that is filled with hopes of life
For the weary and the broken, and the wounded in the strife;
And I offer them the freedom of my great cathedral shrine,
With its sanctity of silence and its fragrance of the pine.

For I crave to be the symbol of the strength that won the fight—
Of the spirit of the heroes who fell battling for the right.
For those dead, who died to save us, let me say eternal mass,
And be God's volcanic voicing of the words: "They shall not pass!"

What most strikes me about Donaldson's poem is the human voice, the consciousness, given to the mountain itself—imbuing it with life. It likewise taints the land in the dysfunction of a man's world, a world filled with murder, war, oppression, and fight.

A few other notable climbs of Mount Marcy include a one-month tent stay by Mills Blake in 1883 while gathering measurements for Colvin's Adirondack Survey, the first winter ascent made by Benjamin Pond and J.W. Otis on March 18, 1893, and a winter ascent from the west in February of 1899 by Gifford Pinchot and C. Grant La Farge.

The Mountains

My first time on the summit of Mount Marcy was July 2, 2014. It was the forty-sixth mountain I climbed in two years to the day. In the first summer of hiking I ascended seven mountains in five hikes: Giant, Big Slide, Gothics-Armstrong-Upper Wolf Jaw, Algonquin, and Redfield (the last an over-night stay with

Neighbor Tom). That winter as I sat and waited for the snows to break, the ice to thaw, for the melt to rush the mountain slides—I found myself reading and studying the region, its history, the people who cared for and lived in it. I discovered the nature writings of Verplanck Colvin, the poetic musings of John Burroughs, read about the findings of Emmons and Redfield, the adventures of Grace Hudowalski and the Marshall brothers.

It was the Marshall brothers who, in fact, set the three stipulations that determine a 46er. The mountain had to hold a summit above 4,000 feet, stand more than three quarters of a mile from the next closest peak, and leave at least three hundred feet elevation gain at the apex. Some mountains that still continue to attract debate include: MacNaughton, known as the "forty-seventh" 46er, which in early twentieth century maps was listed just under 4,000 feet; and Pyramid Peak, that hugs the back shoulder of Gothics about a half mile from its summit.

On Memorial Day Weekend, 2013, once that first winter had come to pass, I set off to climb mountains eight and nine with Jane and Neighbor Tom. The plan was to loop up Nippletop, walk the ridge down Dial, then out over Bear Den and the shoulder at Noonmark, roughly a fourteen-mile hike of about 4,000 feet total elevation gain. (Nippletop is the thirteenth highest point in the state of New York.)

A strange storm rolled in that exact weekend and we found ourselves leaving the Saint Hubert's trailhead in 48-degree, driving rain. I convinced the group to leave our microspikes in the car, thinking there would be no need. But when we climbed the first six or so miles to Elk Pass and the juncture between Nippletop and Colvin the snow was falling in thick cotton-like balls with four inches already draping mountain evergreen. In a view above, white-out blizzard conditions whipped the summit ridge with harrowing intensity. After a heated discussion with Neighbor Tom (who wanted to push on) we turned back. The next day similar conditions and over a foot of snow at Hedgehog summit again turned us away. This time we missed Lower Wolf Jaw.

When one says "46er" does it refer to an individual who climbed all of the forty-six High Peaks or does it actually refer to one of the peaks itself? In reality, they are often one in the same. Without cell coverage or any realistic connection to the outside world an individual's identity inevitably finds itself lost in the wildness of these mountains. The boot rhythms hit with heartbeat, the heart in tune with the mountain's energy. All things here exist in element, or at least how the human mind perceives element. Aristotle claimed there were four: earth, air, fire, and water. Lao-Tzu describes that nothing on earth is as soft and yielding as water, though it is enough to break apart the hard and inflexible. The wilderness continually redefines itself in itself.

The History

There were many important individuals who were local to this region. One interesting person to note: a guide known as "Old Mountain Phelps" who, between the years 1849 and 1869, helped individuals learn how to enjoy the mountain wilderness and the adventures of climbing. The story goes, on a day in 1857, Old Mountain Phelps and his friend Perkins sat on the summit of Marcy and named four mountains on the upper Great Range. I can see the old man pulling a hand through his ravaged, white beard looking across the dramatic fallout at Panther Gorge and all these questions come to mind: was Old Mountain Phelps old at the time? did he yet possess a name that was itself merged with the land he loved? was Panther Gorge yet even named Panther Gorge?

So the story goes, Old Mountain Phelps looked across to the dramatic rockface framing Haystack and thought, that mountain looks like a large pile of hay. And the mountain next to it, its shoulders turning in on itself cupping the landscape, must be named Basin. And the one over there with two humps at the summit, call it Saddleback. And finally, that one in the distance with dramatic spires reaching toward the sky—we should never again say in its presence unless we say Gothics.

Nineteen mountains possess names based on physical characteristics (and thus, metaphor): Haystack, Basin, Skylight, Whiteface, Gothics, Nippletop, Giant, Saddleback, Panther, Tabletop, Rocky Peak Ridge, Hough, Big Slide, Upper Wolf Jaw, Lower Wolf Jaw, Sawteeth, Couchsachagra, Cascade, and Cliff. Up the southwest shoulder of Gothics the pitch is so dramatic there is a weather-beaten, old metal climbing cable drilled into the rock.

When the Marshall brothers were in the midst of their own climbing adventures they also often visited with a man named Mills Blake. Colvin's death in 1920 ended a companionship of forty-eight years with Blake. During the famous survey work of the 1870s, Blake served as main assistant with a title, Divisions of Levels, and accompanied Colvin up hundreds of mountain ascents in every weather condition imaginable. And the Adirondacks have always been known for the extremest of conditions. Blake and Colvin together were known to have run a tight ship for though the work was grueling, it was important. Blake Peak is listed number forty-three in order of height, standing at 3,960 feet above sea level, and remains one of four mountains that actually holds a summit under 4,000 feet. The other three are Cliff Mountain (3,960), Nye Mountain (3,895) and Couchsachraga Peak (3,820).

On June 12, 2014, East Dix, the forty-second highest mountain in the region, was officially renamed Grace Peak in honor of Grace Hudowalski (1906-2004)—the ninth person and first woman to climb all forty-six of the Adirondack High Peaks. (Grace Peak is only the second mountain to be named for a woman.) This grassroots movement was in the works for more than a decade as the U.S. Board of Geographical Names does not look fondly upon changing the names of mountains given the rigmarole required in data change and documentation. Only when enough people continue to use the new name, only when enough of a movement exists to put pressure on the board, will the mountain name change. It is as democratic a movement as one I can think of, with a little bit of protest to boot. Perhaps it is as democratic as preserving beautiful land for citizens and public use.

Part of the Grace Peak movement—which also included an attempt to rename South Dix to Carson Peak—generated a documentary directed by Fredrick T. Schwoebel in 2013 with Summit Pictures titled, *The Mountains Will Wait for You: A Tribute to Grace Hudowalski.* Grace spent decades as Historian of The Forty-Sixer organization, nurturing its community of hikers through a continued personalized correspondence with each person who contacted the group. At any given time Grace might have found a stack of a thousand letters on the table in the living room next to her typewriter. It was Grace Hudowalski's personal belief that to preserve the land we should write about our experiences in it.

The Wilderness

Of the forty-six peaks, nineteen mountains are only accessible via herdpaths. These summits—what the DEC calls "trailless peaks"—contain herdpaths kept and maintained by the Forty-Sixer organization. These trails have no blazes and are often marked with cairns—carefully placed piles of stones that alert hikers to a shift or change in the trail. These herdpaths exist (Neighbor Tom once said while climbing up the slide of Macomb) because people like us actually hike them. Each boot step in dirt shapes the way. The mountain both offered and damaged at the same time.

Most trails up mountains follow one of two paths: either they climb a moderately pitched shoulder along a ridge toward the summit (as in the southern approach to Dix from Hough or the southwest climb up Gothics) or they stay low inside the gut of the mountain where depressions in bedrock have been carved by falling water and erosion (as in the hike to Street and Nye or the trail from Lake Colden to the juncture between Algonquin and Iroquois).

The High Peaks region can really be defined as a gigantic rock rainforest and the ecosystem though extreme offers a shocking diversity of things to see. On the northface approach up Street Mountain one will find a trail draped and adorned in moss (literally, every single rock and depression and tree covered in moss). At the summit of Santanoni or on the ridge toward Iroquois a hiker remains virtually hidden inside tight, thick Balsam fir that cannot grow more than maybe ten feet because of the continual intensity of wind and weather. Above the treeline in alpine zones on peaks like Skylight and Algonquin and Marcy the mountain grips tiny plants and trees—many that are endangered due to the brief growing season.

Even though this ecosystem exists because it works, with enough wind and rain intense storms can often loosen the substrate to the point that an avalanche of tree and moss and mud and rock begins crashing down the mountainside. When the storm finally clears, slides streak rockface like newly formed scars. Hurricane Irene, from 2011, is responsible for a number of new slides in the Adirondacks. Some spots that offer dramatic views of High Peak slides include: from Big Slide looking south toward the Great Range, view of Dix southeast from the Dial-Nippletop ridge, (and my favorite) from Wright hanging over Avalanche Lake with an open rock-filled panoramic view south toward Colden.

The Presence

In the midst of hiking the 46ers I would frequently come home and visit with my folks, retell stories of adventure, often adding the most breath-taking details just because they enjoyed it so much. I imagined my father climbing the mountains vicariously

15

inside these stories, while my mother with wide eyes would first share her concern I might fall off a mountain then plead with me not to hike alone. In the end, they would both ask me to be careful.

My mother, longing to experience the world alongside me, would almost always ask why I do not take pictures. And each time I would explain how I write poems and that other people have a gift for photography, how photography was their way of seeing the world. Somehow, I knew my inability to see the angles with the vista of composition in the right light would have me fussing about the woods in frustration, having to manage a growing sense of urgency. It was a more fruitful experience for me to allow those walking rhythms to claim their own music, hearing the words to rise to surface and the images to take shape in the imagination. Eventually, I would hear the fleeting music and a poem would always come.

For years at Thanksgiving at my Uncle Andy's there was an interesting man who would often visit and, unbeknownst to me, was a well-known Adirondack photographer. His name was Nathan Farb and he lived in the town of Upper Jay. Nathan's career began in New York City (as Andy tells it) immersed in the street photography of the 1960s, where artists would look to capture chance encounters with people in public places. Near and around this time of his life he also taught at Rutgers University. Eventually, however, he settled in Upper Jay into a new kind of immersion—the beauty of Adirondack wilderness. In Nathan's photographs of the natural world he attempts to explore not just the peace and awe of landscape, as he once told me, but also to see the world too in all its scientific beauty.

On a November night in 2012, after my own discovery of the region thanks to Neighbor Tom, I sat the entire evening at Thanksgiving enthralled with Nathan's photos of streams smoothing moss-laden rockbeds near ponds adorned by reeds and wildflowers in blue sky with great distant rocks and views of slides and peaks from the jagged cliffs on mountain lookouts. Each photograph took me back to a hike, each sparked an intense longing to return to the hills.

That year Nathan offered me a small house on his property if I ever felt the urge to stay an extended period of time. Two summers later I took him up on the offer and spent over a month writing and climbing. Five hikes later I had finished visiting each of the 46er summits.

Nathan's images inspired me to question whether language could actually journal these experiences. Journal and journey both variations from the Latin *diurnum*, meaning day. And like a photograph, language too is a translation of experience: the words sometimes a choice among hundreds, the images how they bestow the words with life, the sentences ever-evolving thoughts into motion that move a reader into the mysterious spaces of metaphor and imagination. And the days, always different, always deepening circadian rhythms.

The language of hiking too has its own rhythm: bedrock, trailhead, washbowl, mountaintop, evergreen, cliffwalking, landscape, trailwalking, ridgewalk, somewhere, trailless, waterproof, headnet, everything, songbird, herdpath, payoff, ridgeline, blackflies, lookout, crisscross, mountainside, timberline, moleskin, trailmarker, snowmelt, rainforest, sunlit, northeast, broadwing, bootsole, Haystack, Skylight, Whiteface, Nippletop, Redfield, Saddleback, Tabletop, Armstrong, Sawteeth.

Mountain names, at least here in the High Peaks, are categorized in one of three ways. In one instance the delineation precedes the mountain name as a title, for example, Mount Marcy. For the other two it comes after as a qualifier as in Blake Peak or Basin Mountain. (Of the forty-six High Peaks, only three do not have any delineation or title: Sawteeth, Nippletop, Gothics.)

The only mountain of the forty-six peaks, according to Carson, that has an unclear origin for its name is Dial Mountain. Its summit stands at a large rock that hangs over a ridge at 4,020 feet above sea level about two miles northeast of Nippletop and offers a spectacular view north to the Great Range.

The Ethic

Not counting Old Mountain Phelps and Mills Blake or individuals like Bob Marshall and Grace Hudowalski, who stand as outliers to many categorizations, four other mountains were named after local citizens: Esther, Nye, Allen, and Porter (Nye, a guide, and the latter two doctors from Keene Valley area).

Carson writes, "Esther Mountain, which is northerly of Whiteface, is the farthest north of the major Adirondack peaks. Its northern slope descends on the road between Wilmington and Franklin Falls. In 1839, a family by the name of McComb lived on this road at the foot of the mountain. Esther McComb, a fifteen-year-old daughter, had an ambition to climb Whiteface, but her parents were unwilling. Disregarding their wishes, one day Esther started out alone to make the climb. She reached the top of the mountain now bearing her name, but became lost before getting to Whiteface. A searching party was out all night and found her the next morning. Her mother jokingly called the mountain Esther because of the occurrence, but the name was taken up and has remained" (96-7).

It is difficult to really know how to treat these mountains. Over a two-day period on Labor Day weekend, 2016, some fifteen hundred people hiked Cascade trail from Route 73. The following summer DEC officials rerouted the trail to decrease accessibility. In December, later that year, a young couple needed to be airlifted after getting stuck for two harrowing nights in snow and wind and cold after falling nearly a hundred feet off the summit of Algonquin. And rescue efforts in recent years have increased. The Adirondack Backcountry Hikers page on Facebook (formerly the Aspiring 46ers page) holds over 17,000 members, nearly twice the number of persons who have hiked all the 46ers in total since the Marshall brothers finished in 1925.

And so, the Adirondack Mountain Club offers summer internships for summit stewards, a handful of individuals who climb each day to the tops of the more popular and accessible peaks to offer information to hikers about the delicate—and highly endangered—alpine ecosystem. It is a classic tragedy of the commons: to use and enjoy nature puts great strain on the health of the land and the finite resources contained in it.

When Colvin completed his survey work in the 1870s he actually burned a few of the summits in order to get clear calculations. Cascade is one of these examples of a bald summit just under 4,100 feet in which the ecosystem never regenerated. But overuse of trails and wilderness in the High Peaks region have also contributed to what conservationists see as a legacy effect, where trail erosion and invasive species again return the conversation as to how human beings have affected the environment.

This is certainly a modern tension between humans and the environment (thinking of Aldo Leopold and his thoughts of a developing "land ethic"). From the very early moments of childhood people are born into a life of consumption. The political, social, and economic systems in place that surround them exist in such a way that it proves virtually impossible for individuals not to consume. And this driving force of human living directly harms on a daily basis the very essence of environment. An ecosystem is defined by balance, and when that balance is challenged, it evolves. But humans, now in a period of our natural history called the *Anthropocene*, continue to affect the environment so rapidly and in such drastic ways that the environment simply cannot heal itself.

We now live in a time that can conceive points of no return. Climatologists suggest we have maybe forty years to minimize the ill-effects on the atmosphere. We create more trash now than at any point in history. And there are cities around the globe where lights are never turned off. One feels guilt just being connected into the system. And yet, how can the system be changed by any one person's actions?

There is a mountain on the Dix range—the thirty-seventh highest mountain in the Adirondacks—that stands at 4,060 feet above the level of the sea, set on a rocky ridge at the crossroads between

Macomb, Grace, and Hough Peak. The last five hundred feet of ascent filled with open rockface and views of the impending ridgeline is some of the most fun hiking I can imagine. At the summit there is a sense of being cut off from the rest of the world, as it's one of the few places in the High Peaks where an individual must climb over other 46ers in order to get out. If mountain names change only when people use them I officially acknowledge within these pages this aforementioned mountain as *Carson Peak* in honor of the late Russell M.L. Carson (1884-1961), a native of Glens Falls, New York, and author of *Peaks and People of the Adirondacks*, originally published by Doubleday, 1927.

Retreat, and a Voice for Wilderness

Hiking through woods I see a bird. It leaps to the tip of a moss-laden rock, looks about—olive-gray back smooth, eye-ring sharp. It stands on stiff legs outthrust, thrush.

In a moment it rises, seemingly without effort, to a low branch and in sunlight the rufous tail turns almost tawny. Though it does not sing for it is early spring and perhaps migration still haunts its circadian rhythms.

The Hermit Thrush looks about, then flies away to denser woods.

The first time I saw this bird—a bird beloved by poets (Thoreau especially)—I did not know what kind of thrush it was. I took the fleeting images of moment and memory into the field guide and examined a host of variables like time of year, behavior, the habitat found in, the faint markings of pattern, shade, and color.

Spending time in a world with names requires this sort of observation. A foot lifts from the ground. The mind registers packed dirt, rocks. The moss hang damp, ferns pushing through. Sensibility remains alert, concentration outwardly active.

But this release also moves me intrinsically inward. Sensibilities challenged as I pull inevitably from them.

If insight does not right away come often there exists a need to mediate the mystery of that which one cannot fully grasp, cannot name.

Consciousness, though, heightens at times like these. It is evolutionary, part of the retreat necessary for discovery.

And even when I do not discover or, when the bird flies off just another drab olive-gray bird, the moment teaches me something about ambiguity and uncertainty.

In the absence of successful deduction is presence. Presence of mind and body. This presence is a retreat from answers and from knowledge, a retreat from all that I believe to know.

And in modern times how fitting one often looks to nature as a source for this retreat. A hundred and seventy years ago that kind of thinking would have been considered the lunacy of backcountry woodsmen or poets, when civilizing instincts were driving individuals into the epicenters of villages and towns and cities.

As we consider now, however, this part of our natural history— the *Anthropocene*—the period that marks the noticeable and measurable environmental impact that can be linked back to humans are we not ever more entangled, is the conversation not ever more convoluted, than perhaps at any point on our timeline?

And if wilderness truly proves an escape from the bustle of city living and quaint suburbia what is it in wildness we seek? And what if we have been disconnected from the land for such a time we no longer possess the innate wisdom needed to live as part of it.

But better than fish or game or grand scenery, or any adventure by night or day, is the wordless intercourse with rude Nature one has on these expeditions. It is something to press the pulse of our old mother by mountain lakes and streams, and know what health and vigor are in her veins, and how regardless of observation she deports herself.

John Burroughs, "The Adirondacks" (1866)

Six years ago amidst planning a roadtrip through New England my buddy Neighbor Tom asked me to come hike with him in the Adirondacks.

I was unfamiliar with this part of New York, a state park accessible within roughly an hour's drive north of Albany. He and his family had been visiting the Adirondacks since he was a child.

If a place could lure an individual with those endearing qualities we often look for in people—the Adirondacks.

There is a ruggedness, an almost mythical wildness, to the six million acres of park land enclosed inside what New Yorkers call the "Blue Line."

Within that park boundary live more than 130,000 permanent residents. And an exponentially larger number of visitors in warmer, drier months when the black flies have done their thing or when the deciduous trees begin to do theirs.

It is home to a section of land called the High Peaks and the well-known "46ers," a group of mountains near and above 4,000 feet in elevation first hiked in the early 1920s by Robert and George Marshall with guide and family friend Herbert Clark.

Here, the highest point in the state of New York—Mount Marcy, at 5,344 feet above the level of the sea.

My first hike was one of the more accessible in the High Peaks.

Giant Mountain stands at 4,627 feet, a three-mile climb from the trailhead at Route 73, and on a sunny day in early July our hiking party left the car for our first Adirondack adventure.

Murphy, the dog, spent most of the next few hours bounding up and down huge boldered cliffs, excited to be out of the house.

His mind probably does not consider the peace of nature, hiking for enjoyment. Sure, there is that sudden rush of sensibility now out of the house. But he also wants to be with the pack, and if the pack takes off to climb up and over this huge mountain, he will too.

The hike offered incredible views of the High Peaks. About a mile up on Giant's shoulder some of the first views hit. Imposing mountains so close to one another, so green and full of stark intimacy. Though the geology of the Adirondack mountains proves ancient—rock millions of years old—the range itself is still ever so slightly pushing upward. And above the treeline on many peaks sit alpine zones that contain a multitude of endangered flora.

Out on the cliffs of Giant walking the rough bedrock, watching the mountain fall a thousand feet over, it is virtually impossible to hold back the rush of adrenaline and I imagine most hikers look toward the summit, scramble best they can higher and higher into bright air.

But Giant also includes a series of false peaks. One rises and rises, feeling that burn deep in the thighs, and at last, a view, only to see more mud, the trail farther back, higher up, to another perceived summit beyond.

From the top of Giant it is possible to see Lake Champlain and the Green Mountains. The day we spent there was marvelous, the view a vista that reached outward into open blue sky. After a late lunch we descended the three miles back to the car.

About a mile from the trailhead I noticed Murphyman slowing down. Figured at first he was just tired. Until he eventually stopped walking, laid himself down on stomach and mud.

I approached him, quickly lifted one of his paws, and found the reason. At the mercy of sharp and cracked bedrock each pad on each of his four delicate feet had been torn open, the wet flesh now caked with dirt and small bits of rock.

It was a harrowing final mile back to the car, a combination of lugging him in my arms, almost taking the two of us over dramatic drops in the trail, coercing him through limping when I no longer had the strength.

The next day we found a kind vet in Glens Falls who cleaned

him up and, with ointment and some baby socks, a few days later Murphy was back to himself.

The quarter century from 1900 to 1925 was epochal in Adirondack Mountain history. Prior to 1911, the woods and waters of the Adirondacks were under the overlapping jurisdiction of the Forest, Fish and Game Commission, the Forest Purchasing Board, and the State Water Supply Commission. In 1911, Governor Dix recommended the consolidation of these departments, and, acting on his suggestion, the Legislature, that same year, created a Conservation Commission and enacted the Conservation Law. Under the Conservation Commission's régime, more has been done to open and preserve the Adirondack Mountains for recreational purposes than in any other period of their history.

Russell Carson, "The Conservation Commission Period"
(1927)

As a child I can remember spending much of my youth outside, from morning to sunset, jumping streams and rock-hopping, searching for frogs and snakes at water's edge, threading my way through clusters of trees in what felt like deep woods, contemplating the sky before contemplation.

When kids play like this they develop at an early age a deep sense of presence. The world comes to them unfiltered and in its right color, moves and rains and smells something both different and the same each time. It is never shared in a sense no one else is watching.

That primordial inclination does not leave an individual. Survival dependent upon wonder, the consciousness of a human life, authenticity. Something always seems to lure sensibility into wild spaces.

At the turn of the twentieth century Carson explains how early advocates of Adirondack wilderness opened opportunities for individuals to enjoy the natural settings of upstate New York. Local organizations like the Adirondack Camp and Trail Club, the Adirondack Trail Improvement Society, and the Association for the Protection of the Adirondacks were responsible for the development and upkeep of access into some of the more remote spaces of the park.

The Adirondack Trail Improvement Society is specifically responsible for building two major trails: the first from Haystack over Basin and Saddleback to the Gothics (what is known today as the upper part of the Great Range Trail) built at the expense of William White; the other a trail up the west side of Noonmark at the expense of Dr. Theodore C. Janeway.

Then in 1925 the 46ers are born.

Robert and George Marshall with Herbert Clark finish a seven-year journey to climb the highest mountains in the region. Many of these mountain summits had remained untrammeled by the boot-presence of people.

Their journey was an epic one that would bring to the region in subsequent years a great number of individuals who would attempt to live similar experiences.

In the next fifty years—mostly during the 1970s and 80s—as popularity for back-country hiking in the Adirondacks increased the region experienced a great degradation in its alpine ecosystem, an ecosystem highly endangered due to its fragile and unpredictable short growing season.

The state alpine region is fewer than eighty acres and includes nearly two dozen highly endangered plant species, many of which can be found on the two highest summits.

In 1989, researchers and ecologists under the direction of Dr. E.H. Ketchledge and with the help of local organizations like the Adirondack Mountain Club and The Forty-Sixers gave valuable resources to protecting this endangered plant ecosystem.

The Summit Steward program—a collaborative partnership among The Nature Conservancy, the Adirondack Mountain Club, and the New York State Department of Environmental Conservation—was part of this effort in which hired caretakers were sent on daily treks to many of the open summits throughout the summer to offer hikers important information on the delicate and highly endangered plant communities, as well as to remind individuals of the importance to stay on packed trails, especially above the timberline.

The partnership strived for habitat stabilization and natural resource management to help preserve the high alpine ecosystem and its arctic tundra-like species.

Before closing this report, I desire to call your attention to a subject of much importance. The Adirondack Wilderness contains the springs which are the sources of our principal rivers, and the feeders of the canals. Each summer the water supply for these rivers and canals is lessened, and commerce has suffered. The United States Government has been called upon, and has expended vast sums in the improvement of the navigation of the Hudson; yet the secret origin of the difficulty seems not to have been reached.

The immediate cause has been the chopping and burning off of vast tracts of forest in the wilderness, which have hitherto sheltered from the sun's heat and evaporation the deep and lingering snows, the brooks and rivulets, and the thick, soaking, sphagnous moss which, at times knee-deep, half water and half plant, forms handling lakes upon the mountain sides; throwing out constantly a chilly atmosphere, which condenses to clouds and warm vapor of the winds, and still reacting, resolves them into rain.

It is impossible for those who have not visited this region to realize the abundance, luxuriance, and depth which these peaty mosses—the true sources of our rivers —attain under the shade of those dark, northern, evergreen forests. The term "hanging-lake" will not be deemed inappropriate, in consideration of the fact that in the wet season a large mass of this moss, when compressed by the hands, becomes but a small handful, the rest of its bulk being altogether water; often many inches deep, it covers the rocks and boulders on the mountain sides, and every foot-print made has soon a shallow pool of ice water in it.

With the destruction of the forests, these mosses dry, wither, and disappear; with them vanishes the cold, condensing atmosphere which forms the clouds. Now the winter snows that accumulate on the mountains, unprotected from the sun, melt suddenly and rush down laden with disaster. For lumber, once so plentiful, we must at no distant day become tributary to other States or the Canadas. The land, deprived of all that gave it value, reverts to the State for unpaid taxes.

The remedy for this is the creation of an ADIRONDACK PARK or *timber preserve*, under the charge of a forest warden and deputies.

Verplanck Colvin, "Ascent of Mount Seward"
(1870)

There exists perhaps an ethical responsibility and a moral obligation to write about history with care—human consciousness always at work to contextualize experience. I often wonder what happens to information withheld or judgment given living in a post-Information world?

History offers relevance when it cleaves from itself the inevitably of mythos. For one can too easily romanticize and thus keep at an emotional distance that which is too difficult to bear.

And still the environmental crisis is an old story. A tragedy of the commons. Survival, dependent upon the actions of others. The growing existential fear that any single one of us cannot save a place or the individual self. And we cannot imagine what is to come.

I also cannot forget the root of retreat inherently holds action in its meaning. And still, to retreat takes us to inaction. Inaction does not necessarily mean progress, though it does not destroy.

In the last year upstate New York has become a place for intense debate between advocates wanting to preserve wilderness and those looking to bring business, industry, and tourists to the ever-waning economy of the region.

The issue remains, for much of the Adirondacks includes delicate wetland ecosystems and, with New York's recent land acquisition of Boreas Pond area, the park agency under the governorship of Andrew Cuomo had, for the good part of a year, been unable to reach a designation as to whether this land should be deemed pure wilderness or should allow for not only the establishment of local businesses but various sorts of outdoor activities including the use of all-terrain vehicles, snowmobiles, motorboats, jet skis, and now even drones.

The Northeast Wilderness Trust is currently attempting to protect (through purchase) a large tract of land called the Eagle Mountain Wilderness Preserve. Acquiring the property will safeguard over three and a half miles of brooks, over 155 acres of wetlands, and secure a critical wildlife corridor between two blocks of publically protected land within the Adirondack Park.

An overwhelming majority of local residents have and continue to show support for more wilderness.

This takes us back to a true American dilemma, one found in the writings of the Romantics. As a nation we were an experiment: citizens who were free. Free to do as we wished, generally, within of course the confines of law and our newly evolving judiciary system.

This theme of selfhood versus the collective identity comes through so clearly for me in Herman Melville's great epic. The story takes place in the very environment where during the last five centuries humans have been able to create perhaps the most destruction—at sea. We see it in Ahab's maniacal revenge plot, we see it in the larger story of humans slaughtering animals for their own progress and benefit. But it also comes to us ever so delicately in Ishmael's metaphor of the monkey-rope—how each of us truly finds one another tied to our bankers, our apothecaries, tied in life and death not only to our closest of friends but likewise to those strangers among us.

So much that comes in the mythos of writers like Melville, Hawthorne, Emerson, Thoreau, Fuller, Douglass, Dickinson, and Whitman still speaks to our present day conundrums—what happens when the personal decision-making of a free individual comes in conflict with the collective good?

There is a painting at the Met in New York City upon which I have gazed maybe a dozen times. It is Jacques-Louis David's 1787 painting, *The Death of Socrates*.

The story of the death of Socrates was told by his pupil, Plato.

In 399 BCE, upon being accused of acts to overturn the laws of the state and of corrupting the youth, Socrates was sentenced to death by drinking a cup of poison hemlock. As Plato tells it in the dialogue of "Crito," he had the chance to flee but instead used his death as a final lesson to his pupils. Socrates was his own executioner.

In David's depiction I see the individual qualities of the human spirit—those of passion, rigor, the pursuit of truth.

In a final heroic gesture the old man sends a forefinger up towards the ether, a penultimate sermon on the nature of life and death and the price one pays for a voice. I also see the old man's right hand reaching for the deadly elixir, the onlookers—some unable to look—pleading for reason. Which leads me to consider also those times when one might scarce find a sense of reason, consumed by the rapture of loss, injustice, tragedy.

And yet, now when I think of the life of Socrates I think of a man who spent his days speaking with those who would listen, a man who recognized that through the communion of souls we might better understand the plight of souls. That through discourse we might one day discover recourse.

But this painting only captures a moment in time. In the end David leaves each viewer alone in the ambiguity of interpretation and one must ultimately find a way to retreat from perspective to translate ideas such as these.

So in 1916, a proposition was brought before the voters of the State as to whether a bond issue for increasing the State holding should be authorized in the November election. By a great majority in New York City, and by a smaller majority over the State, the issue was approved, and the $7,500,000 made available will go far to intrench the interests of the State, and the East, for that matter. For the Adirondacks has become the great pleasure ground of immense numbers of vacationists. To have failed to back up the administration of the Park at this critical time in its existence, would have been a crime to the millions of workers in cities who will never be able to afford the time to go to the great breathing spaces of the West. Democracy, in ultimately recognizing what is best for itself, has again triumphed. And this time, before it was entirely too late.

T. Morris Longstreth, *The Adirondacks*
(1917)

One sunny July morning in the summer of 2013, amidst my own excursions to visit the forty-six High Peaks, Neighbor Tom and I set out on a fifteen-mile hike up and over the Santanoni Range. The ascent followed a herdpath winding up and around a shoulder of Santanoni, to the fourteenth highest point in the state of New York.

Amidst thick Balsam fir facing south and west from a tiny summit lookout vast wetland expanse stretched into the distance and haze of morning. From a perspective over two thousand feet above the land it is difficult to imagine the incredible biodiversity below—a complex ecosystem that proves vital to the region's environment as it filters, controls, and balances the flow of water out of the Adirondacks.

The fern, marsh, bog, swamp. The weight and saturation. The White waterlily that in summer opens like a floating hand, its green pads splaying the water's surface.

Skulking in and out of the cattails it might be difficult to see the American bittern, a streaky brown heron that stalks the shallows looking to strike at small fish and frogs.

Wood warblers too like the mustard-streaked, burgundy-capped Palm warbler nest in thickets of Sphagnum moss spotted with the delicate, purpled orchid Rose pogonia, or the blood pink Marsh cinquefoil, that bloom near midsummer.

Among the wading ducks and diving mergansers, river otters and muskrats feed on fresh-water mussels, and the possible wandering moose that forages in deep water lumbering on long legs like stilts.

From Santanoni one follows the ridge about a mile to a spot called "Times Square" that links hikers to the other two peaks. Panther sits about a half mile climb away and it seems most end the afternoon on that bedrocked summit.

But first one must enter the psychological struggle toward Couchsachraga, the lowest of the 46er peaks at 3,820 feet.

The mountain's name—according to Verplanck Colvin—comes from an old Indian expression that encompasses the vast unforgiving wilderness caught between the Algonquin and Iroquois people.

As a hiker leaves the ridge toward "Couchi," moving farther away from the trailhead and descending more than a thousand feet in elevation, it feels more and more a trek into the wild for in order to get out one must collect the energy and the legs to get back up and over the four thousand foot ridge.

The surprise for us that day as we climbed through the scraggly alpine forest toward Couchsachraga's summit was to find a group of old-timers resting at the top with boots off and lunch sprawled about the rocks.

Two of them were already 46ers, but the third had just finished moments earlier rising to the summit.

Something I did not forget that day was Couchsachraga's missing summit sign.

Many of the 46er peaks hold beautiful wooden signage of the classic New York brown and mustard yellow. These locals told us as of late people were stealing them.

One gentlemen suggested perhaps if these signs included not just the mountain's name but also the return mileage to trailhead maybe people would be less inclined to take them.

The sun disappeared behind the hill across Black Bear Lake, but I kept rocking and thinking back to the crises in the life of these mountains. There had been the *first* crisis of lumbering and wildfires in the 1880s. *Then* the Adirondacks had been saved by creating the Forest Preserve out of state-owned lands, and by adding the "forever wild" amendment to the constitution to protect timber and watersheds. Then, as now, many people felt, "Those wealthy outsiders are trying to lock up the land and limit the lumbering."

The *second* crisis was the tourism and recreation industry. With over 9 million visitors a year, many with money, mobility, and leisure the second home craze had hit hard. Land prices had been rocketing. Developers had been buying huge chunks of land for speculation, commercial centers, or housing subdivisions. At this moment, five such major developers wanted to involve 72,000 acres of mountain land. One alone planned for a small, septic-tank city of 30,000 people!

The solution to this second crisis was the creation of the Adirondack Park Agency. Its action was to produce a master plan for the care and custody of *state* lands; then a land-use and development plan for *private* lands with strict density codes. Both were signed into law by then-Governor Nelson A. Rockefeller. The main purpose of these plans is to protect the parklike atmosphere of the Adirondacks and still consider the economic well-being of its residents.

The *third* crisis, as I saw it, was the public's reaction to this "second saving of the Adirondacks." For the most part natives fear the impact of the new controls, while outsiders welcome them. It truly is a "collision of wilderness."

Anne LaBastille, *Woodswoman*
(1978)

The twenty-first century bears witness to an unprecedented use of natural resources, resources many understand to be finite, limited, and easily eroded away. This crisis of consumption will only intensify given the growing nature of access.

How can anyone preserve wilderness or even conceptualize what preservation means in a post-Information age? Major advancements in technology have changed the way our brains now think. We have continual access to everything—ideas, images, people, perspectives—and so attention always remains first and foremost, *meta*. Thought expounded by thought, approach critiqued through approach, insight convoluted by what feels to be active discourse, reality substituted for hyper-reality.

In a post-Information age any perspective can be legitimized.

How many people actually live inside intricately-moderated, self-constructed echo chambers, secluded in tight little worlds of thought and knowledge where one can think what he to she wants because the individual determines it to be so.

Ironically, when I was a child it was information that was isolated. Everything a person needed could be found in a cataloged, alphabetized world. Grab from the shelf the book of *L* stuff and in that section one could find any idea or thing or event of that letter.

But now information is wikied and fluid and available on the smallest of screens. A person carries the world's history around in a pocket. People use it to connect themselves, continually connected, all the time, to anything known by any person who cares to share it.

Where is retreat in a world such as this?

When Henry David Thoreau left for Walden Pond in the summer of 1845 retreat meant a separation from modern living. One left the town, the village. Left the letters at the post. Removed one's self from the contact of others.

And while, yes, Thoreau did entertain many visitors in his time at Walden Pond, and periodically dropped in to see family and friends, his pilgrimage was one of the internal sort—a simplification of life's values, time spent in solitude, and a reconnecting to place and perspective.

Today, that is virtually impossible.

Many remain on a daily basis adrift and alone in echo chambers of solipsism. Any idea generated can be shared and minds have been conditioned so.

Thoreau's notion of living deliberately feels all but lost in the twenty-first century as an attempt to seek a deeper consciousness no longer proves a journey inward but rather moves individuals into emotional and intellectual spaces outside the self—a new hyper-reality—where one can carefully construct and engineer an identity.

Gazing into computer screens connects enough. There is a trade— the deep shimmer of sunset reflected off lake surface for a picture of a sunset reflected off the lake's surface. (Then, someone likes it.)

People are perhaps less entwined than ever to the physical world of sensibility and thus that much more removed from decision-making. The inundation of information complicates perspective. The result is the sacrifice of detail in data, nuance for expression, presence with affirmation.

I am guilty too, and often feel the need for retreat. How easily one can be amazed at the amount of information to share and see.

The concern remains for those who engage the world not as a form of discourse but to simply reaffirm beliefs. Perhaps this is a natural process of identity-making. People find individuals who are like-minded, then consume what they have to say. It fortifies a sense of self. And if any information challenges an already ego-gratified belief-system one can simply defriend or unfollow.

Happiness dependent upon an ability to tailor information, to isolate thinking in caves of thought, to channel a belief system so as to best support individual need.

An individual's ability to love outside the self cannot exist in an isolating world such as this, where information actually stunts discernment and the natural edification of a collective identity.

Whitman too called for contradiction. Without discourse, only crisis can ensue.

One of the greatest advantages of the wilderness is its incentive to independent cogitation. This is partly a reflection of physical stimulation, but more inherently due to the fact that original ideas require an objectivity and perspective seldom possible in the distracting propinquity of one's fellow men. It is necessary to "have gone behind the world of humanity, seen its institutions like toadstools by the wayside." This theorizing is justified empirically by the number of American's most virile minds, including Thomas Jefferson, Henry Thoreau, Louis Agassiz, Herman Melville, Mark Twain, John Muir, and William James, who have felt the compulsion of periodical retirements into the solitudes. Withdrawn from the contaminating notions of their neighbors, these thinkers have been able to meditate, unprejudiced by the immuring civilization.

Robert Marshall, "The Problem of the Wilderness"
(1930)

I, too, at one point experienced a sort of Thoreauvian journey.

In June, 2014, I spent five weeks in the Adirondacks in a small house (previously built) on the property of family friend and Adirondack photographer, Nathan Farb. The idea was to finish the few remaining 46er hikes, then spend the time alone for writing.

It was not entirely clear from the start what would become of the time spent there, but I was hoping the solitude and aloneness would offer some sort of recalibration, a space to refine life focus.

Fundamentally, however, this kind of retreat would in the end remain temporary for a good many of us. By nature we are social creatures with complex emotions and a deep need to share them with others. While a self-isolation possesses its own healing properties it still ends in paradox, insofar as seclusion and retreat actually offer perspective on how to live with others.

I truly believe it will be the myriad voices and perspectives of this post-Information age that will drive what will ultimately be studied in history as a revolution that deeply transformed human life. They will continue to move us closer in the evolution of a civilizing, moral world.

Though it will exist with unprecedented paradigms of contamination. And how much contamination can one planet take.

In 1962, Rachel Carson suggested we were inheriting a dying

earth. Even those who long to live eco-responsibly, those who resolve to preserve the planet rather than harm it, may still suffer from great ecological angst. (Thinking of Wendell Berry and his 1977 essay, "The Ecological Crisis as a Crisis of Character," in which he claims it is virtually impossible to not live a destructive life in an economy that is ultimately destructive.)

Contamination proves a confusing element of crisis because it destroys slowly, and time is a mental construct of human beings. A person thus holds the mental capacity to imaginatively rebuild destruction.

In the meantime the Red spruce forests of many western-facing slopes in the High Peaks are stunted and dying due to dangerously high levels of polluted precipitation that blow in from lake effect weather corroded by the coal-fired smokestacks of the Ohio Valley and beyond.

In local areas acidity in water supply leaches poisonous metals like lead into drinking water.

Adirondack birds like the Bald eagle and Common loon frequently show up poisoned due to new fish species that have evolved to survive acidic waters. Large amounts of mercury contamination have been found not only in fish but in dead bird specimens.

Each spring a profuse amount of acidity trapped in winter snowpack releases into what's known as "acid shock" which poisons plants, animals, and insects at a time when they are most vulnerable.

According to The Adirondack Council statistics show that more than five hundred lakes and ponds out of nearly three thousand in the park boundary are already too acidic to support plant and aquatic life.

In recent years invasive species too have flooded much of the lakes, rivers, and woodlands of the Adirondacks.

Read about the Emerald ash borer or the aquatic Eurasian watermilfoil, Garlic mustard or the Spiny waterflea. These species are a foreign presence to boreal-like environments and one alone can unhinge the entire balance of what was an otherwise self-sustained ecosystem.

In 2016, person 10,000 hiked each of the 46ers. And for the second consecutive summer the New York Department of Environmental Conservation tried to actively dissuade people from using overly-hiked trails. Rescue efforts with the help of DEC, state rangers, and first aid responders have increased at alarming rates in recent years as more and more individuals flock to extreme hiking in the backcountry of the High Peaks.

This influx of exposure and use finds Adirondack communities and beyond overwhelmingly voicing support for more wilderness. Wilderness helps to filter and control the safety of access—one must approach it with care. Meanwhile park rangers are pushed to the limits as a result of under-staffing, more permits approved, new roads constructed, campsites added then renovated, new restaurants and hotels built.

Public land for the use of citizens is a true compass of American democracy. But to what extent is access sustainable, and where is our recalibration with Aldo Leopold's land ethic?

The environmental concerns that have and are unfolding in the Adirondacks speak not just to the region but to our larger world. Consider Leopold's claim of the scholar who appreciates history as a series of successive excursions from a single starting point to which we return again and again looking for a durable scale of values. But even a set value system amidst a chain of events beyond any one person's control inevitably leads to despair.

In the meantime will the Paris Agreement really save our planet? Who will assist people on how to live a simpler life—the EPA,

DEC, John Burroughs?

One might think the answer remains somewhere in the health of local communities. Give twenty-five dollars a year respectively to The Adirondack Council, The Northeast Wilderness Trust. Donate the same to the Bobolink Project, perhaps join the Audubon Society. And buy shade-grown coffee from Birds & Beans. Still, ocean's rise, fill with plastic. Reefs bleach. Sea ice melts at the rate of glaciers. And cities remain a burning torch of light throughout the night.

The human race consumes at astronomical rates and in the last fifty years this consumption has intensified exponentially. And I live a modern life too, am part of this web of connectivity. How can self-sustaining communities exist in a post-Information age? What relevance does any action have in the moment beyond the fear of what is to come.

Time and again, a bird species that has co-existed with humans for hundreds or even thousands of years has suddenly started to decline. Actually, "decline" is too kind a word; bird populations have tended to crash, and all too often in recent history. What took millions of years for nature to perfect can literally be undone in a single human generation. This has happened repeatedly in our lifetime not only to birds, and not only in New York, but to countless other species around the globe. Global warming and a new generation of chemical contaminants pose threats to humans and wildlife that are every bit as urgent as the alarm sounded by Rachel Carson about pesticides a half-century ago in *Silent Spring.*

Darryl McGrath, *Flight Paths*
(2015)

To live a human life in this world—this ever-modernizing and evolving world—is to live in perpetual contradiction and paradox. Perhaps this same unsettling thought sent Thoreau to Walden Pond then the Maine Woods. The ambiguity, the helplessness, the inevitable meaninglessness could have existed just the same.

And yet, consider how different our lives now compared to those of John Burroughs or Verplanck Colvin or Gifford Pinchot.

These individuals lived in a time when the very idea of preservation was beginning to take flight and they had the foresight to see our planet was worth preserving, that beautiful wild places if not protected could be damaged, even destroyed.

This planet however is already dying.

In our country we have reduced many of our wild places to parks, fragmented forest preserves, national monuments. To see some of the most beautiful sights many must sign onto waiting lists, visit them as tourists. Across the globe poorer nations who throughout history had next to nothing are now eating into their own wild places just to survive. Unmappable tracts of forest worldwide so large they are measured in satellite images have slowly disappeared. Sea ice and glaciers, the same fate. Our planet continues to document the decline of species and biodiversity, while sea level rises and rises amidst global warming temperatures.

Which brings us back to our present day moral conundrum: how does one live when to use is to contaminate, to speak is to strengthen the individual echo chamber, to care is to further understand the tragic nature of a dying world?

Our only recourse is to return to that world.

On my birthday last summer while hiking in the Adirondacks navigating the trail from Esther back to Whiteface I saw a little bird, a warbler, perched at the tip of a Balsam fir, kicking its head back to sing. In late June high in the peaks an entire day can be spent listening to the snap, rattle, click, slight flutter, and swirl of warbler song.

Most warblers show yellow somewhere in their plumage. This one stood out immediately—jet black head cap, white cheek and belly, lightly-feathered spot-streaks marbled to its flanks. This was a bird I had read about many times (somehow knew it the moment I saw it). What a fantastic journey this little bird makes.

The Blackpoll warbler (*Setophaga Striata*) is about fourteen centimeters in length, weighing maybe twelve grams, containing over two hundred separate bones. It has evolved thousands of years into a tiny passerine with a radical annual migration.

In early spring this bird leaves its wintering grounds in South America, hits the Gulf coast, spends about a month flying north over a thousand miles through American heartland, feeding, dispersing, before it then migrates an additional thousand miles in the next weeks to summer breeding grounds in the Adirondacks, Canada, with some flying as far north and west as Alaska.

In late summer months into early fall something triggers in the bird's circadian rhythms and it fuels up, begins a long flight across Canada and the Adirondacks finally hitting the Atlantic coast at New England gathering in huge flocks. When the winds are right, when pressure systems settle in, it takes off launching into an eighty-hour continual flight over open ocean until it reaches the northeastern shores of Venezuela.

The last leg of fall migration for this warbler spans roughly a work week.

The Blackpoll warbler teaches us something about space and time.

A bird with such an amazing journey, and this, the first time ever having crossed paths with one.

The global breeding population estimated at sixty million, one of the more numerous warblers found in boreal forests.

Its migration, recorded with the help of technology, travels nearly four thousand miles annually between two continents.

These animals have evolved because what they do works, nature exists how it is (as Neighbor Tom always says) because it works.

And now we are learning there may be even more warbler species that make similar treks each fall and spring.

These birds, their names, and the various systems and migrations and rhythms at work in our natural environment remind us of consciousness. We can follow the flightpath of a Blackpoll, examine its landfall in spring or the day in September when it leaves. We can study its gleaning behaviors, mating rituals, the organs necessary for its high-frequency chipping songs. We can deduce how such a tiny animal can fly so long and so far. We can marvel at its life!

Unfortunately, just as so one can measure impacts of erosion, contamination of lakes and streams, the influx of invasive species, light pollution, acid rain. One can both study and reckon with the causation at work on the planet.

But to see the larger picture we must first retreat. A higher view, a wider perspective. (Maybe this is why people climb mountains.) And after some time when insights come and perspective has evolved we can descend again to better define the criteria, standards, or expectations we should hold for our communities, our global societies, for one another in this new ever-transforming environment in which we find ourselves.

We must first and foremost account for access. It is part of our environmental crisis. Both the access we have to those wild places still available, as well as the access to information we hold in our minds about them. We must take responsibility, not to disseminate messages, but to build a conscience around how we use and share access. Because it comes to us with great risk.

We know human beings can poison the planet. And though it would be undemocratic to restrict access entirely I believe we can find the balance needed to allow our lives and this planet to evolve, to embrace the evolution of all living things—that which defines our natural world.

All things living evolve, all living things grow. This is fundamental. We must fill too all we do and share with that same spirit of life. It comes with a deep and profound respect for all things living. That humanity, at the core, that truly knows anything worth life deserves dignity. That heart and lifeblood of our virtue ethics.

Retreat fills our well-springs with dignity. Not just for ourselves but for everything around us. Because in solitude one soon forgets the self. Creativities begin anew. Again to grow conscience. And then one might see—on this planet everything must have a space to grow—ultimately leading closer to its end.

Presence, Birding, Hiking in the Woods

Clearings become orchestral, and even the deep forest has its songs. Whoever has heard the whitethroat in some remote valley or the hermit thrush from the deep wood at evening has been bound by invisible strings to the wilderness.

T. Morris Longstreth, *The Adirondacks*

Near where I live there is a great little spot for hiking. It begins at a lake, a small lake, down an old country road that feels as if you'd almost have to be lost to find it. Then, right off the side there it peeks out of the mountain chasm above it.

Walking the trail around, if quiet enough, it's not uncommon to spot a Great blue heron standing almost four feet in height, piercing the water's surface at the other end where a creek empties out into the lake.

There are times when an emptiness takes over me.

It usually begins the same way. No one's around, it's quiet. An urgency sets in. At first it alerts me to something I forgot to do. Soon, turns into something I should be doing. Though I know not what. The sense of it seems big, daunting. Like something that comes in sleep, in a dream. You only get one chance at this life.

Then it passes. And I begin to write.

It begins as a low chant over and over deep in the forest interior. At roadside with car door ajar it stops me—still. I am a visitor in these woods.

Without another soul near I hear a haunting crescendo of rhythm and pitch that ends in a casting off of dramatic discord as the Barred owls disturb the end of night.

Minutes pass and I stand motionless, a hundred yards in distance from the calling raptors, and the wild reverberating in the half light of dawn.

Entering the woods I hear familiar voices.

Off to my right a rustling, the hop and poke through leaves and undergrowth *tzwee tzwee*. Up in the maple canopy a garbled finch song falls to the mossy rocks below. Back between the trees a thrush winds up the little machine in its throat. Behind corners of the lake honk through dried reeds.

Knowing requires memory. It requires a turning away from the moment into a previous, once-experienced thought or feeling. How easily I slip into that logic, that reason, that place where the mind creates any reality befitting circumstance. But I long to resist the urge, to remain here in the presence of that which is alive.

That which is pure instinct, animal, alive.

Presence, from the Latin *praesentia,* meaning being at hand.

A bird in the hand. The bush. That in this world of touch. The space of sound, music, color. The pull of the moment.

How this same world also draws me into the lyric poem, because it too is a kind of presence. A speaker held inside a moment of time.

The lyric poem as celebration before the moment turns to memory. The lyric poem as mourning for those we remember. The lyric poem as longing for that which is ephemeral, transitory, impermanent. And so the lyric poem timelines consciousness.

Time, that which defines consciousness. Memory, that which records time. Fear imagines it, loss.

And so we return to forever remain in the present.

> The drifting cries
> of the hawk silhouette
> slip in and out
> of the tree line
> somehow
> through red maple
> and across the afternoon
> where huge white

gray clouds slide
from sight
to consciousness
not present enough
to remember
but startling enough not
to forget each day
that slowly circles
in and away.
If someone could turn
the sun's cracked
light into rain
we'd have a song
worth almost
two growing seasons.
Each step plants
firmly in the dirt
more stationary
than ever. And all
that's temporary
moves around
the body
and withdrawal
which grips it.

There is a certain quiet that hangs in the trees of morning. Light obscures as much as it reveals, the forest dampens before sinking in. Oxygen rises from moss, from fern, chilling the lungs with fresh wet thoughts that forget the boot and its usual grip, the mud thick with suction and slide.

Entering these mountains is a presence all its own.

Most trails twist and meander through dense conifer forest, over stream, past pond and swampy bog, where the solitary loon remembers daylight. It is a summons as loud as the forest is deep and echoes off ridges thousands of feet above.

When it calls out, chancellor of the forest, giver of light and poet of morning, it may be difficult to see its tawny spotted body perched on the mossy trunks of fallen trees, hidden inside forest green.

The Wood thrush's song comes to us in the form of melody—it is a strain for it is performed—all morning, most of the day, and all dusk, a bird who feels it is his job to entertain the forest.

Down inside the thrush's throat levers and stops shift and click, air vibrates up pipe and syrinx, and the various instruments take their turns. If one listens too closely it is possible to trip on a thick root that long ago grew across the path.

All my life I've been looking for things to teach me how to love. Most were people. Many now (I tell people) are birds.

I hear the knock, knock, knock of a downy on a tree and its *meep meep* of surprise. Our dance is momentary, fleeting.

To love, a coming to terms with that which might always remain just beyond reach. I don't know how to live with that kind of longing. I'm always making.

Teach me to love my visitor self, a transient who enters this world on his own accord and who will ask for nothing which is not given.

Coming out of the woods I hear an agitated bird on the other side of the lake. It flies low sweeping arcs along the water barking some *ke ke ke kek* sounds as it swoops from and to various spots along the water's edge, where large trees and branches have fallen from off the shore into the lake creating outcroppings perfect for perching.

The bird is quite big, maybe ten or twelve inches, with dark and what looks like almost iridescent, blue feathers. Around its neck a thick, white band continues down its belly offering a stark contrast in its coloring.

The bird, I found out later, the only of its kind in our area, is a Belted kingfisher.

Lately, I have been reading poems from the Japanese translated by Kenneth Rexroth. At first it seems there is not too much to get from these short lyrics and it is easy to find oneself reading poem after poem without being completely present in the actual poems. Reading Eastern poetry requires a slowing down and in that slowing down—what is real, what is literal, what is right at hand beyond the metaphoric workings of the mind—moves thought into realms of subtle realization.

Art, for me, had always been about complexity. I could remember writing poems to specifically confound, confuse, obfuscate. Most were left reverberating in the world of metaphor and abstraction. It seemed that's what they were supposed to do. But those poems were conscious of their own abstractions. (Perhaps that speaks more to the writer than the work.)

These poems from the Japanese have their own little magics —layers of sensibility turned outward, inward, delicate images, music, yearning.

I so easily enter that world.

An unexpected warmth
brings dense fog and air hangs
heavy in the damp trees. I listen
for a nuthatch or chickadee
but none are near
your scent remains with me.

Does it happen when the first maple leaf loses its pigment. Does it happen when that leaf looses from the branch, spins, floats to ground. The morning chill dampens the grass and scattered leaves with a cold dew.

How I am always willing to embrace the coming of fall, the coming of the dying season.

The subtle morning is suddenly interrupted with the sound of someone chopping wood high in the canopy. (It isn't far off.)

A Pileated woodpecker grips the side of a tree at over a foot in length. This bird is a shy one and if it catches a movement or a sound will likely make off for other dead trees in the area. Its black body looks painted with thick, white vertical striping that runs from its head down the length of its torso. That, and the white spots on the undersides of its wings, like the mockingbird, create a kaleidoscopic effect of color changing when it flies. Perhaps its most distinguishing feature is its bright red-crested head that slams into the trunk of a tree with the like-sound and force of a sledgehammer.

After a few moments of this woodpecker working into the rotting bark of an oak an entire tree branch falls.

Hiking up a mountain I often consider rocks. I see serrated rocks, rocks with jagged edges, rocks breaking, smooth rocks, stones, boulders, glacial erratics, rocks with ridges, rocks that create caverns, ledges, indentations, rocks stacked, slanted and split, rocks crumbling, falling down the mountainside, rocks discolored by water, rocks washed out from rainstorms, rocks firmly planted in the trail and rocks loose in mud, bedrock, wet rocks, mossy rocks, the starry patterns of lichen painted into the nighttime canvases of rocks.

My boot always wears first on the outer suede and tears where it bends at the base of the toe.

Often, his song happens with surprise.

One moment I find myself navigating rocks and mud, climbing and climbing and ever-climbing the trail, the next I hear him call out into the morning ascent—*tzee tzee zoozee.*

The Black-throated green warbler to the naked eye has virtually no green to his plumage and, for a bird twelve centimeters in length and weighing only nine grams, travels a far distance each year with a migration route in recorded seasons as far south as Ecuador.

With its yellow cap and black beard, its white and black streaked body to gray, some say a more fitting name might be the Birch warbler, for inside a grove of whites and yellows this little bird's presence can be lost in a moment.

Though it has been known to hawk insects on the wing most of the time it spends gleaning—little yellow and black, black and white bird—moving from branch to branch in and out of leaves picking at insects in the tiny crevices of bark.

This bird, like nearly two-dozen other wood warbler species, is a common summer resident of the Adirondacks.

I hike up a mountain stream, listen to its gurgle and fall, tread the way among piles of stones. There are poems in these woods.

This water can trust itself to go by contraries, takes us to the source. And it is from that in water we are from. A spoken song of several voices, a story that runs alongside it. This stream, how it is a long way. It has brought its flute.

The mountain ridge rises out of treeline into sunset. It is a cold, clear night. My fingers are numb but sweat builds inside my coat, the body's machinery clicks and turns and generates its heat.

Walking the bedrock I move quickly toward a lookout I know of hidden just off the trail maybe a half mile down. From here one can view wide expanse, a vista. It is a place to sit in the subtle beauty of the coming night.

These are moments I cherish, moments of refined perception, of hereness, moments of primordial awareness.

Once the sun sinks below the horizon, dusk. The coming night stills, more light than not. A blue to yellow to orange fills the sky. Then, after some time, perhaps the good part of an hour, it slowly turns. What was before more light than dark soon begins to glow more dark than light until the view above takes on a deep purple-blue with only a hue of burnt orange hanging to the western mountain ridge.

How I long to remain somewhere between dusk and twilight.

If on a mountain lookout somewhere in the north country, in snow, on a flannel blanket drinking tea or eating soup, and if quiet enough for just a little time, there is a good chance to spot a tiny bird land on a branch nearby. And though he is a curious little fellow sit still in order to get a good look at him.

A little bird with brown head and a cheek of white feathers lands in Red cedar. Its body, no more than a few inches, is painted cream with tawny flanks. It has wings and tail of a bluish-gray with what looks like perfectly straight thin white lines overlaid and prism-like converging to the tail. Unlike other members of its family, the Boreal chickadee does not sing the same way, calling out a huskier version of its name. Though still it is clad in a good jet beard—its coloring a stark contrast in backdrop of newly fallen snow.

The woods in winter release me.

There is a letting go of self, an otherness that longs to get out. Only in the cold isolation of winter when each step into frozen snow and every fluttering in each dark bough magnifies thought. When breath of iced air reminds the body of delicate tissue inside lung, how the body remains flesh, animal and alive.

At night with a full moon the woods arouse the primordial wild in me. Without leaves on some trees in the clear, cold air the dark forest is aglow with an intense soft light. A light that calms and preserves an alertness in the senses, a light that both obscures, beckons. The bare trees have a thousand limbs and their geometries stretch through the nighttime sky.

We are forbidden from a world such as this. The crucial blood pumping through our veins tells us this, reminds us we are entering an otherplace, a place not of welcome and warmth but of a stark, cold, dangerous actuality.

If snow remains light actually reflects up into the eyes, cuts through trees, and washes moonshadows over all one sees.

Only the cold would drive one home.

We are
the only animals
in these woods
you say

two omnivores
trekking at sunset
through an air
that bites the face
cold having pushed
weeks ago
the purr
of the screech owl
south
of these mountains
coyotes now denned.
My wool liner
sits in the trunk
of the car
and pins prick
at my legs
but I forget quickly
as an almost
full moon
slowly lights up
the forest
the trail
opening through
spruce and cedar
the darkening sky
filling with stars
here
and there
where horizon slips
into a smoldering heat
aglow in a place
remembered
by those
who come to it.

It is late afternoon so I hustle to the trail. In a corner of the lake swimming ten feet in one direction, turning, swimming twenty feet in the other are three ducks, good sized ducks. The male leads the way. His bulky white body and iridescent green-black head tense and alert. Two females with gray bodies and brown heads pull close behind in a disturbed duck dance. Floating in the lake are sections of melting ice so they cannot venture far.

My presence becomes too much and, in an instant, the Common goldeneyes begin flapping wing against water and lift into air. They circle one side of the lake, bank before the trees, and fly right over my head.

Walking is a creative activity. Insofar as choice and consideration play a more significant role than reflection and inhibition. When the mind and body move in tandem, when sensibility extends from the intrinsic to the conscious.

The human spirit longs for creative endeavors because we know at some point all things die.

These steps, these walking rhythms, have their own heartbeat. I can feel the energy of the forest rise through me—legs to groin into chest—here in the stark presence of the living.

This song comes to you from the song before it and that one from the song before that and so on these songs come to us as the world breathes a willingness to return though it could be misadventured or miscarried, still you should hold it in your hands, remember it was once another song, how you listened and listened as one might with a song to learn it with heart, even before the notes each by each floated down through the dark canopy to tear your chest little by little into symphonic fire so the forest erupted into a blaze, a music only you could hear, and the birds know it and your memory forgets it, a useless strain, these thoughts that move forever in and out of the trees, here a beautiful flash of blue, there how iridescent.

He is sitting in a tree. Maybe thirty yards into a field. The tree a sapling, no leaves. Melting piles of snow still settle along a small

56

creek where the sun cannot reach, the creek running straight into the woods. His thick talons, the color of egg yolk, wrap around a thin branch that rises on an angle and gives support to the weight of his heavy tail.

From a distance his white belly gives him away. His spotting, shades of amber, have yet to fill out the plumage which means he is probably a first year male. He sits, preening, pulling his black-barred head out of his wings and feathers only to give a look about the field. When he shifts, pivots, peers in a new direction, his tail catches the light. A mahogany colors the base and slowly fades into a bar of deep black that cuts across all his feathers near the tip. His slate gray wings contrast the brown and new black spots on his back and add texture to his shape.

He leaves his tree, flies up the creek toward this spot (he's curious). At about ten yards he banks, turns, glides to a perch, lands. Bobbing to balance the weight of his heavy tail the American kestrel looks about momentarily, takes off again, flaps his wings, a jarring sort of bat-like flight, hits the woods and is gone.

For the first time in months I fall in love again with rocks. My boots are beaten down and worn from a year of tough Adirondack hiking. Head down, stepping from rock to rock, I climb swiftly, notice again the outer suede tearing where my left boot bends at the base of the toe. The afternoon sun filters through trees, not quite warm. Memory kicks in.

The woods are close. Buds fat, ready to burst. The ground softer. Red-bellied woodpeckers bark at trees. The ferns growing less obstinate.

In a few weeks on the mountain ridge warblers will begin showing up, Pines and Blue-wings and Blackburnians and Magnolias and Black-throats.

Climbing a mountain often pushes me to such physical and emotional limits. The water and mud, insects and rocks, the effort, the mind's continual and sharp concentration, the ever-rising bedrock—it all takes a tremendous toll on the body. And I would be remiss to deny there are moments of doubt.

But once at the summit all presence of being seems to lift into the winds, into the wisp-revolving clouds and, on a clear day, the horizon cuts mountains out in every direction.

This is a fleeting perspective—a rare peek out into the world, a view down into the magnificence of rock and glacier, of ridge and faultline, of water and substrate.

These views are always that of one out into the world. In a present moment we cannot see ourselves standing at the foot of a great precipice, a tremendous slide falling and falling away from our boots, a lone body standing at the needle's eye of a great rock, a mile above and nearly two hundred away from the level of the sea.

To hear its call is as unmistakable as its white throat and tiny yellow eyebrows, as unforgettable as the black and white stripes that begin at the brow and diverge to the back of its head.

A traveler will often hear this sparrow making great racket inside piles of leaves, under bushes, hopping and poking about the undergrowth. But this bird too is an ascender of mountains, he is a peak-bagger, a surveyor of summit views.

To catch its song is to hear a lullaby set forth from the tips of Balsam fir. The first note trills like a pitch pipe moments before the serenade, and lo! then it comes. With its own variation of dactylic trimeter, out of its nest and endlessly rocking, the White-throated sparrow sings poems into the afternoon.

There is a scene in my mind. I see the canvas.

The sky, first blue, with small thick yellow-white upstroke streaks.

The trees, dense and green, some dark green, some lighter where the sun catches the space. They bend and hang over the lake.

The lake, horizontal, dark. With blues and grays and streaks of violet underneath the bright lime green of lily pads. Dots of white for lilies an echo for the eye.

I would want to put a bird in a tree across the lake. No one would know it was there, but me.

These trees and their light confound me

and there is a tanager across the lake. There is a tanager

across the lake and the trees rise into sky

where they begin.

The sky has no beginning, yet ends across the lake.

Where there is a tanager. There is a tanager

across the lake

and I love you more than your words. All my life

these words were all I had, now I look in the birds

for you. There is a tanager

across the lake, I see its light in the trees.

What trees they are I do not know

though trees they are. It is a faraway spot

of scarlet

on green, the most lush green I have seen in months.

The tanager has returned

and brought with it color. There is a tanager

across the lake, it is there because I see it

or it moves

or it sings into this afternoon

at the rocky shore of this lake

when the trees looked as if they could touch the sky.

There is a tanager across the lake, whisper

in its presence, for though it seems to always return

a tanager sits in a tree

across the lake.

Catch it land in a Lilac tree or Bog laurel and its movements are unforgettable. Its tail, long in comparison to the rest of its body, flicks up and down, a balancing act for this acrobatic flycatcher. The large tail necessitates quick dips, turns, dives, ascents to catch insects on the wing.

Its song comes in two parts. The first, an up-down two-beat whistle beginning high-pitched, ending on an off-beat full of slight discord. The second, after a brief moment of silence is a rapid, monophonic fluttering one might expect from a songbird.

With a dark greenish-brown head that blends into a slightly lighter gray-green back, and a light yellow-white underbelly, perhaps the Eastern phoebe could be mistaken for a number of other passerines.

Once extended beyond the boundaries of self out into the environment around us, we imbue it with life. A place where a light breeze lifts the hanging beech leaves into sunlight and a strong tumbling stream lulls into mountain reverie. A place where juncos flit and dart from trail behind large glacial erratics adorned with moss. Even Red squirrels fitful in their noise-making.

As soon as I strip of mud and wet gear, enter the confines of a car, I consider a return.

These birds are all around us, each one with a name.

And the creek carving its history into the mountain is a song. And the kingfisher eyeing the minnow's flash, a song. And the bright green moss that blankets the forest floor, a song. The chime of Wood thrush. Footsteps through newly fallen leaves, songs. Rocks, these songs, the suction and mud. The deep quiet of cedar forest. And these songs of longing and love.

NOTES & FURTHER READING

The book's title pulls from the spirit of John Burroughs, American writer and naturalist, born in 1837 on a farm near Roxbury in Delaware County, New York.

And the epigraph from "The Adirondacks" by John Burroughs, first published in the collection *Wake-Robin* (1871); also found in *Deep Woods* (p.1), edited by Richard F. Fleck (Syracuse University Press, 1998).

On Russell M.L. Carson and *Peaks and People of the Adirondacks*

Original excerpts of this essay are published online with the *Adirondack Wilderness Advocates* (found online at adirondackwilderness.org).

The Adirondacks (p.xx) by T. Morris Longstreth, originally published in 1917 by The Century Co. (reprinted by Black Dome Press, 2005).

Woodswoman (p.7) by Anne LaBastille, originally published in 1978 by E.P. Dutton (reprinted by Penguin Books, 1991).

Russell M.L. Carson's *Peaks and People of the Adirondacks*, originally published in 1927 by Doubleday (reprinted by the Adirondack Mountain Club, 1973).

More on the life of Grace Hudowalski in the documentary *The Mountains Will Wait For You: A Tribute to Grace Hudowalski* directed by Fredrick T. Schwoebel (Summit Pictures LLC, 2013).

Also, please read Annie Dillard's, "Expedition to the Pole," from *Teaching a Stone to Talk* (Harper Perennial, 1982).

Retreat, and a Voice for Wilderness

An original version of this essay is published online with *SAGE Magazine* at the Yale School of Forestry and Environmental Studies (found at sagemagazine.org).

"The Adirondacks" (p.26) by John Burroughs, first published in the collection *Wake-Robin* (1871); also found in *Deep Woods,* edited by Richard F. Fleck (Syracuse University Press, 1998).

"The Conservation Commission Period" (p.247) in Russell M.L. Carson's *Peaks and People of the Adirondacks,* originally published in 1927 by Doubleday (reprinted by the Adirondack Mountain Club, 1973).

"Ascent of Mount Seward" (p.96-7) by Verplanck Colvin, from *Adirondack Explorations: Nature Writings of Verplanck Colvin,* edited by Paul Schaefer (Syracuse University Press, 2000).

The Adirondacks (p.16-9) by T. Morris Longstreth, originally published in 1917 by The Century Co. (reprinted by Black Dome Press, 2005).

Woodswoman (p.240-1) by Anne LaBastille, originally published in 1978 by E.P. Dutton (reprinted by Penguin Books, 1991).

"The Problem of the Wilderness" (p.208-9) by Robert Marshall, from *Bob Marshall in the Adirondacks: Writings of a Pioneering, Peak-Bagger, Pond-Hopper, and Wilderness Preservationist,* edited by Phil Brown (Lost Pond Press, 2006).

Flight Paths: A Field Journal of Hope, Heartbreak, and the Miracles with New York's Bird People (p.282) by Darryl McGrath (SUNY Press, 2015).

For more information found in these pages please see the following resources:

Peter G. Redmond's "Protecting the Islands in the Sky: Lessons from Conserving the High Alpine Communities" from *Adirondack Journal of Environmental Studies* (1997).

The Complete Birder by Jack Connor (Houghton Mifflin, 1988).

Garrett Hardin's "The Tragedy of the Commons" published in *Science* (1968, Vol 162).

"The Ecological Crisis as a Crisis of Character" by Wendell Berry from *The Unsettling of America* (Sierra Club Books, 1977).

A Sand County Almanac by Aldo Leopold (Ballantine Books, 1966).

Wilderness Ethics by Laura and Guy Waterman (The Countryman Press, 1993).

The Adirondack Council (adirondackcouncil.org) & Adirondack Experience (theadkx.org).

Presence, Birding, Hiking in the Woods

An original version of this essay was published in *Platform Review* (ARTS By the People, 2017).

Essay includes an epigraph from T. Morris Longstreth's *The Adirondacks* (p.40), originally published in 1917 by The Century Co. (reprinted by Black Dome Press, 2005).

The following poems: "Hike to Sunfish Pond," "This Song," "Across the Lake," originally published in *L'Amour Fou* (2015), *Platform Review* (2017), *The Piedmont Journal* (2017), respectively.

At one point this essay references (evolved) lines from poems by beloved poets Robert Frost, Li-Young Lee, Marie Howe, and W.S.

Merwin. Please see "West-Running Brook," "Lake Effect," "Prayer," and "Dusk in Winter."

And please read J.A. Baker's *The Peregrine* originally published in 1967 (New York Review of Books, reprinted 2004) which started first in me these ideas for this essay; and Fanny Howe's "Bewilderment" from *The Wedding Dress* (University of California Press, 2003).

Ra Press out of South Burlington, Vermont, and Chestertown, New York, is a small independent press that has been publishing fiction, drama, poetry, and essays of the Adirondacks and beyond since 2000. It began as a literary cooperative experiment in Ticonderoga, New York, then was re-structured into a full-fledged publishing house with its move to Vermont in 2007. Find more books from their complete catalog at the Crow Bookshop in Burlington, Vermont, or online.